W9-AMN-021

Mountain Goats

By JoAnn Early Macken

Reading Consultant: Jeanne Clidas, Ph.D.
Director, Roberts Wesleyan College Literacy Clinic

WEEKLY READER®
PUBLISHING

Please visit our web site at **www.garethstevens.com**.
For a free catalog describing our list of high-quality books,
call 1-877-542-2595 (USA) or 1-800-387-3178 (Canada).
Our fax: 1-877-542-2596

Library of Congress Cataloging-in-Publication Data

Macken, JoAnn Early, 1953–
        Mountain goats / by JoAnn Early Macken. — (Rev. ed.)
              p. cm. — (Animals that live in the mountains)
        Includes bibliographical references and index.
        ISBN-10: 1-4339-2414-5   ISBN-13: 978-1-4339-2414-9 (lib. bdg.)
        ISBN-10: 1-4339-2497-8   ISBN-13: 978-1-4339-2497-2 (soft cover)
        1. Mountain goat—Juvenile literature. I. Title.
QL737.U53M218   2009
599.64'75–dc22   2009000105

This edition first published in 2010 by
Weekly Reader® Books
An Imprint of Gareth Stevens Publishing
1 Reader's Digest Road
Pleasantville, NY 10570-7000 USA

Copyright © 2010 by Gareth Stevens, Inc.

Executive Managing Editor: Lisa M. Herrington
Senior Editor: Barbara Bakowski
Project Management: Spooky Cheetah Press
Cover Designers: Jennifer Ryder-Talbot and Studio Montage
Production: Studio Montage
Library Consultant: Carl Harvey, Library Media Specialist, Noblesville, Indiana

Photo credits: Cover, pp. 1, 15, 17, 19, 21 Shutterstock; pp. 5, 9, 13 © Alan and Sandy Carey;
p. 7 © Michael H. Francis; p. 11 © Tom and Pat Leeson

Printed in the United States of America

1 2 3 4 5 6 7 8 9 14 13 12 11 10 09

Table of Contents

Boldface words appear in the glossary.

Cute Kids

A baby mountain goat is called a **kid**. Soon after it is born, a kid can stand. It drinks milk from its mother.

kid

In a few days, a kid starts to eat grass. For about a month, it drinks milk, too. It stays with its mother for about a year.

Kids push and chase each other. They hop off high rocks. They learn how to climb.

Nanny Goats and Billies

Male mountain goats are called **billies**. Female mountain goats are called **nannies**. Both nannies and billies grow horns and beards.

Mountain goats eat grasses and plants. They swallow their food quickly. Later, they bring it up and chew it again. The food they chew again is called their **cud**.

Mountain goats climb well. They balance on thin ledges. Their feet grip the rocks and ice.

Life in a Band

Nannies and kids stay in groups called **bands**. An old nanny leads each band. Billies join them in winter.

Mountain goats live high in the mountains. The weather is cold up there. Heavy coats help keep them warm in winter.

In spring, mountain goats lose their thick coats. They rub against bushes. They rub off their winter fur.

Fast Facts

Height	about 3 feet (1 meter) at the shoulder
Length	about 5 feet (2 meters) nose to tail
Weight	Males: about 300 pounds (136 kilograms) Females: about 155 pounds (70 kilograms)
Diet	grasses and shrubs
Average life span	up to 12 years

Glossary

bands: groups of mountain goats

billies: male mountain goats

cud: food that has been swallowed and brought up to be chewed again

kid: a baby mountain goat

nannies: female mountain goats

For More Information

Books

Alaska Animal Babies. Deb Vanasse
(Paws IV Children's Books, 2005)

Mountain Goat. Zoo Animals (series).
Patricia Whitehouse (Heinemann, 2002)

Web Sites

Mountain Goat

*animals.nationalgeographic.com/animals/mammals/
mountain-goat.html*
Print out your own mountain goat fact sheet.

Mountain Goat Facts

idahoptv.org/dialogue4kids/season3/mt_goats/facts.cfm
Watch a show about mountain goats from Idaho Public
Television.

Index

About the Author

JoAnn Early Macken is the author of two rhyming picture books, *Sing-Along Song* and *Cats on Judy*, and more than 80 nonfiction books for children. Her poems have appeared in several children's magazines. She lives in Wisconsin with her husband and their two sons.